News and Messages

*A messenger brings
a letter to a lady.
A painting by a 17th
century Dutch artist,
Gerard Terborch*

News and

Line drawings by
Peter Reid

Messages

Muriel Goaman

DAVID & CHARLES
NEWTON ABBOT

ISBN 0 7153 5661 5

Copyright © MURIEL GOAMAN 1972

All rights reserved. No part of this publication may be
reproduced, stored in a retrieval system, or transmitted, in any
form or by any means, electronic, mechanical, photocopying,
recording or otherwise, without the prior permission of
David & Charles (Publishers) Limited

Set in 13 on 14pt Bembo
and printed in Great Britain
by Redwood Press Limited
for David & Charles (Publishers) Limited
South Devon House   Newton Abbot   Devon

Baron Reuter (page 42)

Opposite: Policeman using
walkie-talkie (page 54)

Previous pages:
left, 19th century town
postman (page 37)
right, 18th century
country postman

Contents

To
Anthony Rogers

*Egyptian hieroglyphic
writing, 16th century BC*

The Need for Communication

I

CAN you imagine what it would be like if we had no way of expressing our thoughts to other people? If we could neither talk nor read and write? If there was no radio, television or telephone? It is difficult to visualise such a shut-in existence.

All our living is communicating with others. Some people learn to communicate easily. Others are more withdrawn, and find it hard to make approaches to people whom they do not know. This is why it is so helpful to learn to express our thoughts clearly; it opens up life for us.

Early man lived a tightly closed existence. He could cry out and grunt. He could point, and make other gestures, but in the beginning he had no language.

Probably he noticed the animals which were all around him. You yourself may have seen some of the warnings that animals give each other. The jay, that brightly marked species of bird which belongs to the crow family, has a harsh cry. When the jay is disturbed in a wood it flies screeching through the trees, alerting other woodland creatures. The rabbit stamps its hind feet before scampering off to shelter, and

An alphorn blower in Switzerland

shows its white scut (tail), giving warning of intruders. A bear cub up a tree comes running down when the mother bear calls it by thumping on the tree trunk. Worker bees go out from the hive as scouts, to find flowers that contain nectar; then they return to the hive and hover in a sort of dance that tells the other bees where they can find these flowers.

Early man perhaps picked up the idea of making simple signals from the animals he watched. But after a while he found that signs and grunts were not enough. Gradually he matched signs with sounds, so that by the time thousands of years had passed, man had developed speech. Now he was different from the animals; he could talk and get a reply.

Primitive man's problems were not over when he had developed speech. He still had to learn how to communicate with other people who were a long way off. At first, he

8

probably depended on a loud voice. Certain tribes used to post men on hill-tops, ready to shout warnings to each other when their enemies appeared. Julius Caesar (100–44 BC), who invaded Gaul (now France), found that wooden towers had been built to shelter such men.

Swiss cowherds in the Alps learned to make their voices carry across the mountains by yodelling. This noise is made by singing or shouting alternate unnaturally high notes and deep normal tones. The cowherds also make their voices carry by using a long curved horn called an alphorn or alpenhorn.

When the Europeans started to colonise America, they found that the North American Indians had trained their voices so that they could talk to each other over very long distances.

From early times, farmers hung bells round the necks of the animals in their flocks or herds, so that they could be found easily. We know that this was the custom in Ancient Rome. It is still carried on today in some countries.

Bells have long been used for signals. During times of national danger, such as when a great plague or fire occurred, church bells rang out to warn the people. This alarm signal was known as the tocsin.

After the Norman Conquest of England in 1066, William the Conqueror began the custom of having a bell rung every

Cows wearing bells in Switzerland

evening, warning the people to put out their fires and go to bed. This bell was called the curfew, from the French words *couvre feu* meaning 'cover fire'. In those days most of the houses were made of wood and there was no chimney, just a hole in the roof to let out the smoke. There was great danger of fire breaking out at night, and destroying a whole town, unless the citizens were careful to put out their fires.

During World War II, church bells in Britain were not allowed to be rung. This was in case of an invasion by the Germans; the sound of church bells was to be a sign that the Germans had landed.

Drums have been used since prehistoric times. The earliest type of drum was probably a hollow tree trunk, with fish or crocodile skin stretched over the open end, Messages could be sent many miles in this way, especially if the drum was played near a river, as water is a good carrier of sound.

Woodcarving from Ashanti, Ghana, showing a West African drummer

At first hands were used to beat the drum, and a system of signals was developed, long and short drum beats all having special meanings.

Later, drums were covered with animal skins, and were beaten with sticks. Messages sent by drums from one African native village to another have been called the 'bush telegraph', a term which came into use in the first place in Australia.

Tom-toms, or tam-tams, were first used in India. Today the name is taken to mean the sort of drums that are used for sending messages by any uncivilised tribes.

Drums have been used in the British Army for hundreds of years. They were used to beat a retreat, to beat an alarm, to beat up recruits, and so on.

Man has developed many ways of using sounds to send messages. If he needs help, a hunter can fire a shot from his gun to show where he is. Sailors use rockets, maroons and sirens. When a fire is reported at the fire station, an alarm is set off to call in the firemen. A train whistles to show that it is coming. Cars have horns. Factories have hooters which mark the times to begin or finish work. These are just a few examples of how man makes use of sound.

So far, all these messages have been those that can be heard. Early man also discovered ways of sending messages that did not depend upon sound at all.

One of man's earliest warnings was the beacon fire on a hill-top. As the first one was lighted and flared up, the beacon on the next nearest hill was started, until there was a chain of beacons blazing for miles around. In this way news of approaching enemies could travel far more quickly than the enemies themselves. In the sixteenth century when the great ships of the

Spanish Armada were sighted as they approached England, beacons were lighted all along the coast warning the English fleet under Sir Francis Drake at Plymouth that they must be ready to fight.

Smoke too can be seen from a long distance. The American Indians would light fires and then damp them down so that smoke was produced. They could control the number of puffs of smoke, and the space of time between the puffs, working out many different messages which their friends, miles away, could understand. In those early days when the Europeans landed in America and took land away from the Indians, probably one of the most frequent smoke messages sent was 'Sharpen your tomahawks! Palefaces are coming to harm you!'

On a sunny day light can be reflected from a shiny surface. This use of reflected light is an ancient signal probably as old as beacon fires. During World War II sailors and airmen carried shiny steel reflectors in their escape kits. Then, if they were wrecked or shot down, they could direct light flashes to help their rescuers.

Early man wanting to show the path through a forest would chip off pieces of bark from some of the trees he passed. The word 'blaze' in the expression 'to blaze a trail' has nothing to do with fire; it means the white mark left on the tree, resembling the blaze or white mark on the forehead of some horses. Sometimes woodmen leave piles of stones on a forest path to show the way they have gone.

The Stars and Stripes

The Union Jack

Every country has its national flag. The British flag (sometimes called the *Union Jack*) is made up of three crosses: St George's for England (red cross on white ground), St Andrew's for Scotland (white diagonal on blue ground) added by James I, and St Patrick's for Ireland (red diagonal on white ground) added in 1801.

The flag of the United States of America (sometimes called the *Stars and Stripes* or the *Star-Spangled Banner* or *Old Glory*) consists of thirteen stripes representing the original thirteen states (alternately red and white), and fifty stars (white on a blue ground) representing the fifty states of the union today.

In ancient times, flags were carried into battle. When a knight was enveloped in armour with an enclosed helmet he looked just like any other knight and was unrecognisable by

Medieval knights jousting, with heralds blowing trumpets. From a 14th century manuscript

his men. So he wore a surcoat over his armour, embroidered with the same emblem as that of his flag, or standard. His men could recognise the flag, and could follow their leader easily.

Flags have a language of their own. For example, the Royal Standard flies whenever the monarch is in residence; the Union Jack flying at half mast indicates that some well-known person has died.

Ships use an international code of signals, by flag, light and sound. Seamen know these shipping signals by heart, so that they can act on them without hesitation.

Semaphore, which has a special semaphore alphabet, is a method of signalling with flags or lights which was employed a great deal by sailors before the morse code and the telegraph were invented. It is useful when, for the sake of security, radio silence has been ordered.

On motorways warning lights flash on overhead indicator boards to warn motorists of any danger ahead, such as fog, ice, an accident, or other hazard.

Queen Elizabeth II touring south London. The Royal Standard is flown on cars when used by the monarch

2

Man Learns to Read

WE have seen some of the ways in which early man sent simple messages. He was unable to send written ones because he had no alphabet. The invention of the alphabet is one of the greatest steps forward that man has ever taken. From it, he has been able to develop all forms of learning, to exchange ideas with men of other countries, and to write down and explain great discoveries and inventions for the use of future generations.

Of course the alphabet did not just happen. It was not invented by any one man. It came about, over many thousands of years, by slowly developing from picture-signs, and from symbols which stood for different words. When man started to link certain sounds with certain symbols, writing became possible. Messages from then on could be sent in the form of written letters, carried by special messengers or couriers. The illustration above, of a runner delivering a letter, is based on an early 14th century manuscript in the British Museum.

One of the most famous of early messengers was called

Assyrian account of the flood, in cuneiform writing on a 7th century BC clay tablet from Nineveh

Pheidippides. He was a Greek courier, who used to run with messages for the army.

In the year 490 BC Greece was at war with Persia. In September of that year, the Greeks won a battle against the Persians. Pheidippides, already exhausted from running many miles here and there with messages, was sent to tell the Greeks at Athens that the Persians had been defeated. He had to run a distance of over twenty-two miles to bring his message of victory. Having gasped it out to the eager Athenians, Pheidippides fell down at their feet, dead from exhaustion.

It may seem strange that we should remember Pheidippides in these days, but there is a good reason for this. The battle which he died to report was fought at Marathon. Since that day, any great test of endurance is called a marathon. Pheidippides used to compete at the ancient Olympic Games, which were held every four years, in July. After centuries during which the Olympics were allowed to lapse, they were started again in the year AD 1896. A marathon endurance race was introduced then, and was won, suitably, by a Greek.

One of the earliest ways of writing was to use a pointed reed (a stylus), which stamped out letters in wet clay that was then dried in the sun. The letters written in this way were wedge-shaped, and are called by the Latin name for this, *cuneiform*. This form of writing was in use about 3000 years BC.

Early Egyptian writing was in hieroglyphs, a kind of picture-writing in which each separate character (or letter) was made in the form of a different little picture. Hieroglyphic writing eventually became more simple. The ordinary man had not the time to draw all those beautiful pictures to make words. Only the priests could write in true hieroglyphs, which were used in sacred carvings. These can be seen on ancient temples in Egypt, and on the Rosetta Stone in the British Museum in London. There is also hieroglyphic writing on the obelisk called Cleopatra's Needle on the Thames Embankment, London, and on a similar monument in Central Park, New York, USA. Both of them were brought from Egypt during the nineteenth century.

Later the Egyptians found out how to make a sort of paper. They took reeds called papyrus which grew on the banks of the Nile, and cut them into strips, which were

Egyptian hieroglyphs on Cleopatra's Needle, a granite monument of about 1500 BC brought from Alexandria to London in the late 19th century

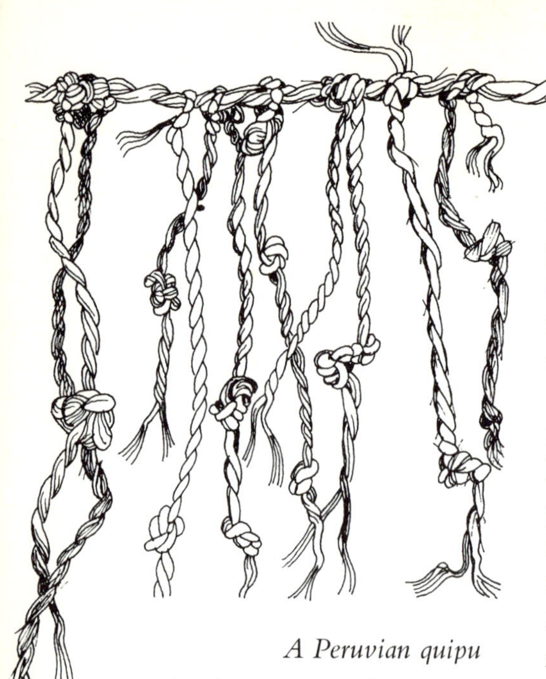

A Peruvian quipu

then gummed together and pressed. After they were dry, they were rolled into a long scroll. The word papyrus gives us our own word paper.

Before the days of throw-away tissues, linen or cotton handkerchiefs were used. Your parents may have tied a knot in a handkerchief to remind them of an urgent message or appointment. The name for a memory-aid is a 'mnemonic'.

Early man used mnemonics in exactly the same way as a knot in a handkerchief. He used knotted cords called *quipus;* the name comes from Peru in South America. All sorts of ingenious records and messages could be kept or sent by the use of quipus. One large main cord had thinner cords joined on to it, spaced at intervals. Knots were tied on these thinner cords, each knot having a special meaning. The cords were coloured; red for soldiers, green for corn, and so on.

The early Roman messages were scratched on wax tablets, with a sharp pen called a stylus. A messenger could smooth the wax and thus rub out the message if the enemy caught him.

The North American Indians sent messages on birch-bark, or on wampum-belts made of beads and shells, arranged in definite patterns on animal skins.

Most of the messages of olden times were carried by couriers from the army to the battle front, or through the lands of

18

conquered people. It was a long time before the idea came to man to send messages of peace.

Carrier pigeons have been used for thousands of years to carry messages. At the starting ceremony of the Olympic Games of the Ancient Greeks, a flock of pigeons was released to tell the nation that peace must be kept during the period of the Games. When the Olympics were revived at the end of the nineteenth century, pigeons were released before the Games began, as a symbol of peace. This usually forms part of the opening ceremony at each Olympic nowadays.

Pigeons have carried messages, and still do, in both peace and war. Often this has been the only way in wartime to get a message through. Pigeons are used, rather than any other bird, because they have a strange power of finding their own way home; another name for them is 'homing pigeons'. They can be taken miles away and when released they fly straight back. The message, on thin paper, is tied to the carrier pigeon's leg.

Wampum belt of North American Indians

The messengers mentioned so far carried their messages all the way from the sender to the receiver. The journey might have been a short one during just one day, or it might have taken months to complete and have covered hundreds of miles. It was not until the idea of a relay system was developed that long-distance messages could be carried more quickly.

Cyrus, king of Persia in the 6th century BC, worked out a good relay system. He built roads, and arranged for his couriers to go on horse-back just as far as a horse could travel easily. At each stage fresh horses and men were waiting. Night or day they could carry on the message a stage further. A famous Greek historian who saw the Persian messengers said of them, 'Neither snow, nor rain, nor darkness is permitted to obstruct their speed.' After many years of war the Persian Empire came to an end, and their system of sending messages was temporarily forgotten.

The growth of the Roman Empire brought a great advance in communications. By the end of the 1st century AD five main roads had been built across Europe, all leading to Rome. When the Romans colonised Britain (AD 43–410) they built similar roads all across the country. These roads were necessary not only for the movement of troops, but also for sending messages.

The Romans built posting stations at intervals of about ten miles along these roads. Here we get the origin of our word 'post'. We tend to think of the post as the letters and parcels which we send and receive. The original meaning was a fixed post or station, where couriers and horses were changed. The posts were supplied with lodging houses, where couriers could rest after their journeys. When the road ended at a river or at the sea, boats were waiting for the couriers, who were rowed on to the next post. Anyone who interfered with the couriers or their messages was executed.

With all these early postal relay systems it was only the letters of kings and emperors which were carried. There was no postal system for the private citizen. Indeed, letter writing by the few people who were able to write in those days was discouraged. The rulers feared that it might lead to plotting against them. If any messengers carried private letters for a friend, they did so secretly and against the rules.

The ancient Roman Empire, over-run by barbarians, gradually fell into decay. There was no one left to use the posts in Europe, and for hundreds of years they were forgotten.

Principal Roman roads in Britain.
The names are post-Roman

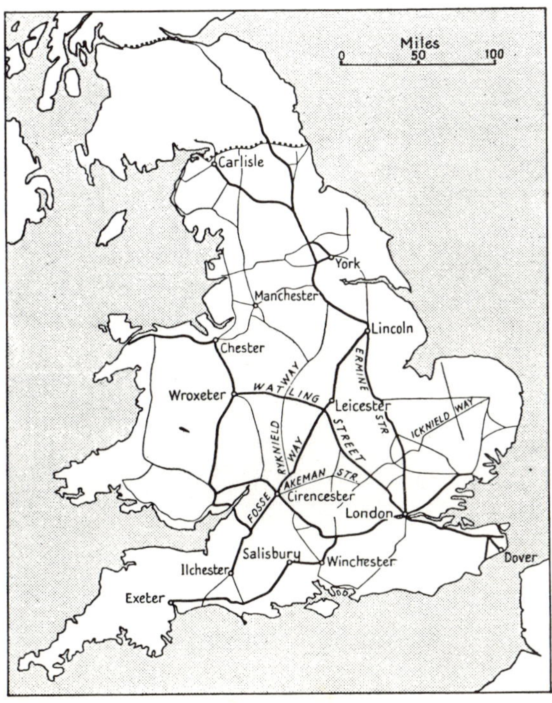

3

Books and Printing

In Ancient Egypt books were in the form of papyrus rolls; they were rolled up with the writing on the inside. The Greeks followed the Egyptians in the use of papyrus rolls, and later the Romans adopted them. Our own word 'volume' comes from the Latin *volumen*, meaning a roll.

The libraries of those days would seem strange to us. There were no neat rows of books with gay covers, but many long or short rolls, tied round the middle. To read one, you would have to unroll it and lay it out flat. The longer the roll, the more cumbersome it would be to read. You would have to roll up the part you had just finished and unroll a bit more as you went along.

Sometimes leather was used instead of papyrus; leather was

Above: 16th century printing works in Holland

followed by parchment and vellum, which are stronger than papyrus, and can be cut into larger sizes; more important still, the writing can be on both sides. The art of book-making thus improved greatly. It was now no longer necessary to join the leaves together into a long roll. Parchment and vellum leaves were folded and bound on one side, or along the top. The book could be unfolded and read all along one side, then turned over for the other.

At the time of the fall of the Roman Empire, monasteries were already firmly established in many countries. They managed to survive the Dark Ages which followed, when books and learning seemed to be forgotten. Part of the daily work of the monks was to copy manuscripts. They produced extracts from the Bible, and from various religious works. They sometimes copied books on such subjects as history, philosophy, mathematics, law, medicine and so on.

Many of these books, on parchment or vellum, were beautifully illustrated with gold and coloured lettering, and with tiny

A monk at work on an illuminated manuscript. The illustration is itself taken from an illuminated manuscript of the 14th century

24

pictures in the margins. They are known as illuminated manuscripts. The monks laboured over this work for long hours, often in unheated cells, and with no artificial lighting. As you can imagine, each book took a very long time to complete.

The monasteries kept in touch with each other, sending messengers around in the different countries carrying letters on parchment scrolls. These letters became a sort of news bulletin; each abbot would read the letters to his own monks, and would add local news at the end. The scrolls became longer and heavier at each stop.

The ordinary people who were unable to read could understand stories told in pictures. The early Christians realised this, and they decorated the insides of their churches with pictures showing stories from the Bible. Some of these pictures were painted, and have worn away with time. Others were made of mosaic (tiny pieces of coloured marble and glass fitted together).

11th century mosaic of the Crucifixion from the church at Daphni, Greece

Paper-making in the 16th century. Moulds are being dipped in rag pulp and the sheets laid out to dry

China was a highly developed country when Britain was still almost totally uncivilised. Two thousand years ago, paper was made in China from rags and bamboo. For almost a thousand years no other country discovered the secret of paper-making. Then in the 8th century AD, some Arabs living in Samarkand in Asia were invaded by the Chinese, and took some Chinese prisoners. The Arabs learned the art of paper-making from their captives, and carried the knowledge into Europe. Gradually the art spread, until paper was used more often than vellum in the making of books.

In those days, paper was made from linen rags. This material supplied enough paper for the number of books that were being produced. However, as more people learned to read and the demand for books increased, other materials were sought. All kinds of fibres were used—flax, esparto (a strong grass), straw, old rope, and so on. The supply of material started to run out.

A Frenchman called Reamur (1683–1757) made an important contribution to the art of paper-making. He was a keen naturalist, and one day he noticed some wasps chewing dead wood. He watched and discovered that they plastered the pulped wood into a sort of greyish-white paper and built their nest from it. So man copied the insects and started using wood-pulp for making paper. Since the middle of the 19th

25

century most of the pulp used for paper-making has been produced from trees.

As the Chinese were producing paper a thousand years before it was known in the west, it is not surprising that they also invented printing hundreds of years before the Europeans. The Japanese and the Koreans also practised the art at the same time as the Chinese. They used wooden blocks on which were letters in *relief* (raised above the surface). A block was inked and then paper was rubbed against it. The Chinese alphabet consisted of thousands of different little picture symbols or characters.

It is thought that the first mechanical printing press to use metal type was invented by Johann Gutenberg in Germany in 1455. The first book known to have been printed from movable type, and called after him, was the Gutenberg Bible; although undated it was probably produced in the same year. William Caxton (1422–91) was the first printer to set up in England.

Printing in Europe was invented at just the right time for the expanding need for books. Plenty of paper, of good quality, was available. New universities were being founded in the larger cities, and more and more people were learning to read.

Up to that time, books had been so rare and precious that Bibles were chained to the benches in churches so that readers could not take them away. The coming of printed books meant that many copies of each book were produced instead of just one, and therefore they were much cheaper. For the first time they came within the reach of people who had never been able to afford them before. The written word now spread ideas farther than ever.

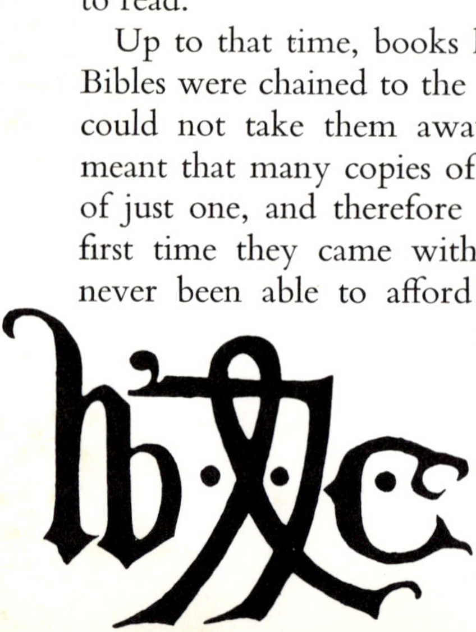

Caxton's signature

The chained library at Hereford Cathedral

There will always be people living amongst us who, for one reason or another, cannot read books as we do. The blind, for instance, would never be able to read with ease had it not been for a Frenchman called Louis Braille (1809–52).

Louis was the son of a cobbler; as a small child he used to play in his father's shop. When he was only three years old he picked up a sharp tool and tried to punch a piece of leather with it. The tool slipped and ran into his eye. As a result of this accident the other eye also was affected and he became completely blind.

When he was ten years old he gained a scholarship to the National Institute for the Young Blind in Paris. Valentin Haüy, the school's founder, taught his young pupils to read embossed (raised) type with their fingers. This was a very slow and tedious method of reading; writing by it was more difficult still.

A French artillery officer, Charles Barbier, produced a system of embossing dots and dashes on card, which he called

A blind girl reading by feeling the raised dots with her fingers

(Below) The Braille alphabet

'night writing'. His idea was that by using it soldiers on the battle-field could write and read messages during the hours of darkness. In 1821, Barbier took his system to Haüy's school, where Louis Braille showed great interest in it. He realised that the perfect system of reading for the blind lay somewhere between Haüy's embossed books and Barbier's complicated dots. For many years Braille worked on a system that used a

1st LINE	A	B	C	D	E	F	G	H	I	J
2nd LINE	K	L	M	N	O	P	Q	R	S	T
3rd LINE	U	V	X	Y	Z	and	for	of	the	with
4th LINE	ch	gh	sh	th	wh	ed	er	ou	ow	W

six-dot code until he had produced the quickest and simplest way of reading and writing for the blind, which is called Braille after him.

Many other ideas have been developed to make it possible for the blind to read and write, but nearly all of them were devised by people who could see and who were therefore unable fully to understand the difficulties which face a blind person. Louis Braille's system, now used all over the world, is probably so successful because it was devised *for* the blind *by* a blind man. Today there are libraries for the blind, from which adults and children can borrow books and magazines produced in Braille.

One of the first typewriters ever known was invented in France in the 18th century for embossing letters to be read by the blind. This machine was possibly made for the pupils at Haüy's school. In the United States a man called Burt of Detroit invented a typewriter in 1829, calling it a *typographer*. The earliest typewriter believed to have been actually manufactured and sold to the public was Hansen's 'writing ball', invented in England about 1870-5.

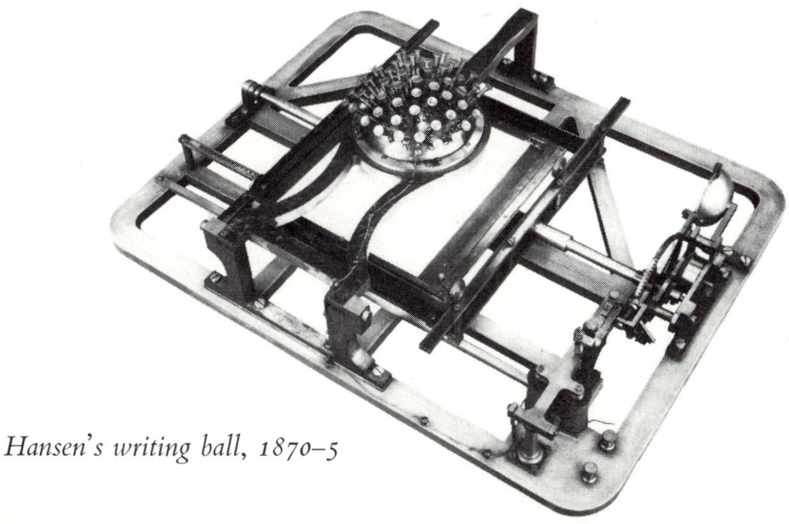

Hansen's writing ball, 1870–5

4

Carrying the Mail

AFTER the fall of the Roman Empire, almost the only messengers to be found in Europe came from the monasteries. Much later, as trade began to increase between towns, messengers were needed to carry business letters for the merchants. A postal system grew up in part of Germany soon after 1239 which lasted for about four hundred years.

Universities, too, needed messengers. Some of the students came from far away, and wanted to send letters to their families. Kings had their own messengers, who used to wear a livery (special clothes provided by one's employer). In England, the royal messengers wore scarlet trimmed with gold. Cities and towns started messenger services for business connected with running the affairs of the town.

There were official messengers everywhere, all travelling for their own employers, but there were none for the ordinary people. Sometimes private messages were carried secretly. After a time this practice was encouraged, and a fee was charged for the service. Only the wealthy could afford to use it. Poorer people used to send letters by travelling friends, or by the pedlar. He called at their homes, selling pots, pans, ribbons, clothes, purses and many small objects that a modern housewife could find in the shops. Unfortunately the pedlar might not pass that way again for months, by which time any reply that he might bring would be out of date.

Successive English kings set up relay posts in times of emergency; these lasted for a short period, and then dwindled.

During the reign of the Tudor King Henry VIII (1509–47) the first *Master of the Postes* was appointed. Brian Tuke (later Sir Brian) re-established the ancient postal relay system, dividing the roads into stages. His job was to see that accommodation was provided for the messengers and post-horses, and to keep the delivery of letters flowing as smoothly as possible. Later the rate laid down for the charge of post-horses became one penny per mile.

The messengers were called post-boys. They carried the royal mail in a leather bag, and they each had a post-horn.

16th century post-boy

Opposite: Medieval pedlar

This was a long straight brass horn, which they had to blow three or four times every mile, and also whenever they met travellers or came to a town or village. The post-houses where they stopped for food and a change of horses were all inns. A sign showing a post-horn hung over the door of every post-house. Thus the inn-keeper became post-master too. He took the local letters from the postbag, and handed the boy more to deliver.

The post-boys were badly paid, and apart from the excitement of their arrival at a posting-house, they had a lonely and dangerous journey. Roads in those days were deeply rutted cart-tracks, full of pot-holes. In the winter they were either frozen over or thick with mud. In the summer, dust coated the hedges as the post-horse trotted along. Sign posts were unknown then, and it was very easy to get lost. Worse still, highwaymen often lurked behind copses or bushes which grew beside the road. Many post-boys were attacked and robbed of their mail, which sometimes contained money.

Envelopes were unknown in those days. A letter was written on a sheet of paper, which was folded over so that the four corners met in the middle. The rectangle so formed was then folded in half, with the points inside. The address was written on one side of the new fold. Holes were pierced through the folded ends, and a thread was passed through the holes, then twisted all round the letter and sealed with wax on the back.

Houses of that period were not given names or numbers. People who had businesses in towns

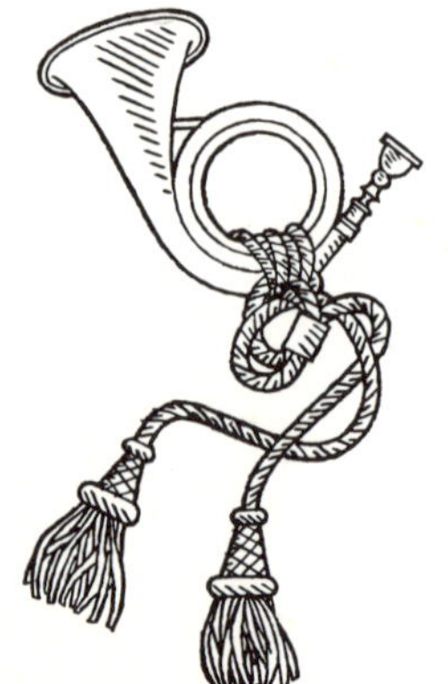

A post-horn

usually lived over them, not in a house somewhere else as so many do today. Few people had any address at all, as we know it. This rather complicated the addressing of a letter; sometimes there was scarcely room left to write all the words. An address might have read something like this:

To his esteemed kinsman James Grosse, Gentleman, at his house hard by ye sign of ye Fleece Inn, Glocester.

In fact, letters were delivered to a post-house, and had to be collected from there.

Although the post-boys travelled all over Britain, they did not carry local mail in London. People living in the city who wanted to write to each other had to deliver their letters personally or pay special messengers.

In Paris in 1653, the French King had authorised a postal service by which letters were carried at the cost of a sou. A man called William Dockwra, in London, may have known how successful this scheme proved to be, for a little later he introduced a similar service in London. Each letter, prepaid, cost one penny, and the service came to be known as the

A highwayman

Hyde Park Corner, London, 18th century, showing a stage coach and a waggon with wide wheels to help it through the mud. The milk maid is having a chat

London Penny Post. At first, Dockwra lost money, but soon he began to make a profit. Immediately, the British Government took over the service, which became part of the general postal system.

During the 17th century, the stage coach became the main means of travel across England. It was a clumsy vehicle, usually without springs, pulled by four or more horses, and travelling at about four miles an hour. There were posts every twenty miles or so, where the horses were changed.

Roads in Britain were still in a bad state, and often the coach became stuck in a pot-hole. Although highwaymen did attack stage coaches at times, they seemed safer than post-boys who were travelling alone. People began to send their mail by stage coach, which was against the law.

34

In 1784, John Palmer, a theatre-owner of Bath, suggested that a special mail-coach service should be established, running between London and Bath. The new mail coaches were a great success. Not only did they travel fast for those days (seven to ten miles an hour); they also carried an armed guard who sat at the back, above the level of anyone else in the coach, with a good view all around it. He wore the royal uniform of scarlet and gold, with a high hat, and blew his post-horn at intervals.

The Post Master General was responsible for providing the guards and coaches, while the coachmen and horses were supplied by contractors, often the inn-keepers who kept the post-houses. The mail-coach services lasted for about sixty years, until the first railways took over their work. In spite of the success of the coach system, there was general discontent at the high postal charges.

The British Government was not interested in complaints by the public. Many years earlier Parliament had passed a Bill voting itself special exemption from paying for the carriage of mail whilst Parliament was in session. This privilege still exists; modern Members of Parliament can send letters to their constituents (electors) free of charge from the House of Commons. In early days, however, this practice (then known as franking) had become widely abused.

In 1748 Parliament decreed that all franks must be dated and the letters posted on the same day. (From then on, franking came gradually to mean what it does today, that is, the addition of special marks, instead of stamps, to parcels or letters, to show that postage has been paid on a certain date.)

It is understandable that the ordinary people resented having to pay high postal charges when wealthier Members of Parliament paid nothing. Postage in those days was charged per sheet, double for two sheets, treble for three sheets, and the basic cost depended on how far the letter was carried. The further away from the writer, the more it cost. It is not surprising that letters were written closely all down one side of a sheet, then turned and written across, so that some of the words were almost cancelled out.

In 1835 Rowland Hill (later Sir Rowland) began to collect information about the British postal services; he got little help, as officially his questions were unwelcome. He found that Irish labourers working in England were unable to keep in touch with their families at home because of the expense of postage. He heard that Coleridge the poet, when staying in the Lake District, had seen a young girl look at a letter from the postman and then return it to him, because she could not afford to pay him. Coleridge insisted on paying for it. When the postman had gone, she confessed to Coleridge that she and her brother regularly corresponded with each other by marking certain dots on the back of the letter. They were a code which told each of them all they wanted to know, and was their own secret way of franking.

19th century postmen on centre-cycles, which were nicknamed 'Hen and Chickens'

Rowland Hill realised that the cost of a letter, to the Post Office, could be divided into 3 parts:

1 for receiving the letter and preparing it for its journey;
2 for carrying the letter from Post Office to Post Office;
3 for delivering the letter and collecting the money.

In a pamphlet which he produced on the subject he urged the Government to introduce the Penny Postage System for all inland letters; this would mean that the cost of sending letters would depend on the weight of the letter (and not on the number of sheets or the distance of the journey), and that the uniform minimum rate would be a penny. Instead of the recipient paying the postage, Rowland Hill suggested that the sender should pay, by using 'stamped labels'.

After four years of argument, Parliament agreed to the scheme, and Penny Postage became established. Not everyone approved; the Marquess of Londonderry, hearing that letters would be delivered to his home in future, asked 'Am I expected to cut a slit in my mahogany door?'

Rowland Hill was asked by the Government to work out the details of his scheme. He needed a wrapper and a label. To bring in plenty of ideas for their design, he held a public competition. The label became the first adhesive postage stamp. It bore a design of Queen Victoria's head, and was known as the Penny Black.

The Penny Black, issued on 6 May 1840

A gazetti coin

5

Newspapers

NEWSPAPERS did not begin only when the printing press was invented. They had been appearing for hundreds of years before that, and had taken many forms.

In Ancient Rome, Julius Caesar ordered that public announcements and notices of interesting events should be written on a white board and displayed in the Forum (the central gathering place), where anyone passing could see them. This became a sort of news bulletin, and was called the *Acta Diurna* (doings of the day). Romans who lived far from the centre of the city sometimes employed scribes to copy the news for them.

We have seen how, in the days when few people could read, the monks of Europe used to send messages to their brother monks in other countries. These letters sometimes contained important news of great battles, famines, plagues, coronations of kings, deaths of prominent people and so on. The letters were almost like news sheets; they were carried from one monastery to another, or from one nobleman's household to the next. Truth and rumour were mixed up, because often there was no way of verifying the stories.

Kings and people in authority used to pay for news to be sent regularly to them; in this way they were forewarned if there was an uprising, or other threat to their safety.

In 1563 when the Venetians and the Turks were at war the Venetian Government produced a monthly newspaper, written by hand. This was read aloud to the people in various public places in Venice. A *gazetta* (a small Venetian coin) was charged for hearing it read. This gave us our word 'gazette'; the first official English newspaper was called *The Oxford Gazette*. It was published by the court of King Charles I, then established at Oxford, at the time of the Civil War (1642–6). Each side in the war, both Royalist and Parliamentary, published weekly news-sheets attacking the opposite party violently, and often telling untrue stories of what was happening.

North-east side of the Forum in Rome, as it was thought to be in Julius Caesar's time

When Oliver Cromwell came into power after the beheading of Charles I, he banned all the news-sheets which expressed opinions that he disagreed with, and *The Oxford Gazette* was suppressed for a time. After the Restoration, when the monarchy was restored and Charles II became king, the court returned to London from Oxford and *The Oxford Gazette*, re-established, changed its name to *The London Gazette;* it is still published today, and gives official Government news.

About twenty years before the Civil War, printed pamphlets began to be sold in England. They were called *corantos* (meaning 'running' that is, part of a series of papers) and they were translations of foreign pamphlets, telling of news abroad. They were strictly censored; nothing could be printed in England without a licence—no news-sheet and no book. Anyone who wrote articles which critised the way the English Church or State was run was liable to be punished. Some offenders were placed in the pillory; this was a contraption with a wooden frame attached to an upright post. The prisoner had to put his head and his hands through holes in the frame, which was locked into position. He would be left there for several hours while passers-by jeered at him. The constable would stand near him, to tell the people what his offence had been.

The pillory was not abolished in England until 1837, but from 1815 it was used mainly for punishing offenders guilty of perjury (giving false evidence on oath). In Delaware, USA, the pillory was a legal punishment until 1905.

The Star Chamber, the Court that inflicted penalties in England for publishing without licence, was abolished in 1641, but it was not until the end of the 17th century that

The pillory

Englishmen were permitted to print and publish whatever they wished, without having to get permission from the authorities. Even then the publishers of papers had to be careful not to criticise politicians, for fear of action for libel. However, their readers were evidently deeply influenced by the writers, and the Government must have feared this influence, for in 1712 a tax was put on newspapers.

Some famous writers were being published in the papers of those days. Daniel Defoe was one of them, and he was pilloried and imprisoned for his writings. In later years he wrote many novels including *Robinson Crusoe*.

The newspaper tax hit most of the better newspapers because they could no longer pay their way. Bad papers survived the tax, for politicians used to bribe unscrupulous editors and publishers not to criticise them in print. Thus newspapers in England became corrupt and worthless, because truth had been sacrificed for money. When newspapers started to print advertisements the publishers were able to become independent, and the tone of their papers improved.

41

Illustrations in those early days were woodcuts. When photography was developed this new form of printed picture was used.

The main newspapers today have their own representatives in foreign capitals, and also correspondents in the main provincial towns in Britain, who telephone the editor if any unusual event occurs. If necessary, reporters can be sent to the spot.

Reuter's agency was the first to print foreign news. It was founded by the German P. J. Reuter (pronounced Royter) in the mid 19th century. An enterprising business man, Reuter tried to set up business in Paris, but there were too many government restrictions. He came to England and became a

The London Post, January, 1646

Mid 17th century newspaper, with woodcut illustration

Reuter kept some of his pigeons at this inn in Aachen, Germany. Here a pigeon is being sent off in his memory by Reuter staff

naturalised British subject. At first he sent private messages for firms by the newly invented telegraph and where no cable had been laid he used pigeon post. Sometimes he even laid his own cable where none existed, and he was thus able to report on the progress of the American Civil War before ships bringing the news could reach England. The main news agency in many countries today is affiliated with Reuters, a name which is known all over the world.

Early newspapers used to have the letters $^{N}_{E\ ^{S}\ W}$ printed on the front page, to show that the information in them was collected from the four quarters of the globe. The inventor of the symbol evidently overlooked the fact that he had placed the compass points E and W in the wrong places! It is true, however, that in our modern newspapers we do get news from every country in the world. One of the most important ways of receiving and passing on information is the Press Conference of today. The Prime Minister prepared to give his reasons for wanting to take Britain into the Common Market; the Leader of the Opposition ready to explain his own attitude

43

to this; great athletes who have broken sports records; pop stars with hundreds of teenagers adoring at their feet; astronauts who have returned safely after landing on the moon and driving a buggy across its surface; some other famous person who has caught the eye of the public; any of these can invite reporters to meet them, or can be invited by the Press to come along to a Press Conference. This gives the reporters the chance to put the sort of question that the man in the street wants to ask; and the person interviewed can say exactly what he feels. The questions may be difficult, or even embarrassing; sincerity comes across, just as falseness and evasion show up clearly. Both question and answer may be found in the next issues of the newspapers. The modern Press Conference keeps the ordinary people in touch with their governments, and with those who represent them to the rest of the world.

Press conference of astronauts Aldrin, Armstrong and Collins (left to right) of Apollo 11, when men first walked on the moon. In quarantine, they spoke to reporters by closed circuit television

6

Telegraph, Telephone and Radio

Man has always been trying to perfect his system of sending messages. His dream has been to be able to talk to someone thousands of miles away just as clearly as if he were in the same room at that instant. The development of the use of electricity has made this dream a reality.

During the eighteenth century, scientists of many nations experimented on different types of telegraph. When we talk, our voices send out sound waves, which can be sent along a wire, changed into electric waves, and shown on a machine. For a long time scientists had realised that if those electric waves could be changed back to sound waves at the receiving end, then voices could be heard clearly.

One of the most famous names connected with the invention of the telegraph is that of Samuel F. B. Morse (1791–1872). He was an American portrait-painter, living at Boston in the United States. He became so interested in the idea of an electric telegraph that he gave up his post as Professor of Sculpture and Painting at New York University, to devote all his time to his research.

A ·—	M ———	Y —·——
B —···	N —·	Z ——··
C —·—·	O ———	1 ·————
D —··	P ·——·	2 ··———
E ·	Q ——·—	3 ···——
F ··—·	R ·—·	4 ····—
G ——·	S ···	5 ·····
H ····	T —	6 —····
I ··	U ··—	7 ——···
J ·———	V ···—	8 ———··
K —·—	W ·——	9 ————·
L ·—··	X —··—	0 —————

Morse code

He invented the morse code, a system of letters, numbers and punctuation marks, all represented by dots and dashes or a combination of both. If you are a Guide or a Scout you probably know the morse code, and use it for signalling with flags or lights. Samuel Morse sent his dots and dashes along a wire, and worked for many years, improving his system. He was unpaid, and at times was hungry and penniless.

Morse tried to get the American Government to contribute to the cost of the first telegraph line. It took five years for Congress to vote the money, but in 1843 Morse was able to construct a line 40 miles long, from Washington to Baltimore. In May 1844 the first message in morse code was sent on the line, four words from the Bible: 'What hath God wrought?'

Morse hoped that his success would influence the Government to finance and run the telegraph, but they turned down the idea. It was left to private investors to develop, and it proved to be highly profitable. His code has been adapted for international telegraphic use.

Many scientists realised that it should be possible for telegraph wires to be laid under the sea. Samuel Morse foresaw the laying of a submarine cable across the Atlantic. He experimented with a cable in New York Bay, but was unsuccessful. The difficulty with early cables was to find the right form of insulation.

46

The sea floor has to be surveyed carefully before a cable is laid, and in shallow water, rocks and any sharp objects such as old ships' anchors and wrecks must be avoided. In 1850, a cable was laid under the sea between England and France. It broke very soon after it was connected, but a year later another cable was laid, between Dover and Calais.

The transatlantic cable was a more difficult problem. In 1857, during the first attempt, the cable broke whilst being laid, and was lost. The following year, a cable was laid between Ireland and Newfoundland; this lasted for a few months, then this, too, broke and was lost. In 1866 the famous steamship the *Great Eastern* successfully laid a cable between England and America. Today cable ships travel across the world, laying and repairing cables.

The submarine cable which was used for transmitting telegraph signals by morse code was invented long before the telephone; far more complicated apparatus is needed for sending speech along wires than for sending morse code.

Machinery on board the 'Great Eastern' for paying out the Atlantic cable when it was laid in 1866

Many inventors were working on the idea of a telephone at the same time. Alexander Graham Bell (1847–1922), a Scot who, like Morse before him, also lived in Boston, was the first man to achieve success.

In 1876 Bell was working with his assistant, Thomas Watson. They had a workshop in the cellar. Bell went up to the attic with part of his newly completed telephone, and said quietly into it, 'Mr Watson, come here. I want you.'

Watson, listening through the apparatus in the cellar, heard the words clearly. Filled with excitement, he rushed upstairs. 'I heard the words,' he told Bell. No one had ever sent a verbal message over a telephone before.

When an inventor produces a new idea which shows promise, he usually applies to his country's Patent Office. There he is granted *letters patent* by the crown or government; this gives him exclusive rights to make or sell his invention for a given number of years. The letters patent are designed to prevent anyone else from stealing the idea and making money out of it.

Bell filed his application for patent for his telephone only a few hours before one of his competitors put in a claim to apply for a patent for an electric telephone. Other inventors claimed to be first in the field, and many law-suits followed. It was agreed that Bell's application was the first, and he was granted exclusive right to sell his telephone.

As with so many other inventors, Bell had spent years perfecting his instrument, and had borrowed money from friends. Even when he produced his telephone, the general public was not very interested in it. 'Who would want to speak over a telephone?' was the common reaction. However,

the Bell Telephone Company was formed, and developed into a great success.

Bell's first telephones were let out in pairs; only the two people sharing the telephone could speak to each other, and over only a few miles. The telephone was crude, and very unlike the instrument we know today. There was no telephone exchange until 1878.

Many great inventors have made their contribution towards the development of modern communications. They built on the knowledge passed on by others. In the sphere of radio (originally called wireless) the name of Guglielmo Marconi (1874–1937) stands out.

Marconi was an Italian. From the age of twelve he was interested in chemistry and physics. He was determined to find a way of sending signals through the air without using wires. When he was twenty he achieved this, and by the end of the following year he was able to transmit his signal more than a mile.

The young Marconi photographed soon after his arrival in England in 1896, with his apparatus for 'telegraphy without wires'

Marconi offered his invention to the Italian Government, but they turned it down. So he left for England, where the British Government saw possibilities in it. In 1897 a British company was formed to develop wireless telegraphy. One of its great benefits is that ship to shore communication can be made when there is no other way of sending messages across the sea. Many lives have been saved by ships' radios.

In the early days, the distress signal was the three letters SOS. It was thought by some people to mean *Save our souls* or *Save our ship*, but in reality the letters were chosen because in the morse code they are simple to signal, being 3 dots (S), 3 dashes (O), 3 dots (S). In 1909 radio distress signals at sea were used for the first time after a collision between two American ships, the *Republic* and the *Florida*. The lives of 1,500 people were saved, and the public awoke to the great value of radio at sea.

The SOS signal is still used by ships; in addition, the spoken

50

word *Mayday* (from the French *m'aidez*, help me) is used on the ship's radio telephone.

At the beginning of this century, many keen amateurs had taken up wireless telegraphy as a hobby. Those who could not afford to buy a set built up their own from component parts. Their numbers grew so rapidly that they caused interference with government and commercial radio, and eventually the amateur receiving stations had to become licensed to operate.

In 1920 these amateur operators were excited when they heard that Marconi's company in England was going to broadcast music for one hour each evening for two weeks. This was the beginning of the regular radio programmes which we enjoy today. In 1922 the British Broadcasting Company was formed, later to become the British Broadcasting Corporation. Today it is frequently referred to as the BBC.

Our radio sets today keep us in touch with many of the things which are important to our way of life; not only entertainment, but also weather forecasts, news, time-checks, traffic reports and so on.

Think of all the people who rely on weather forecasts:

Operators at work in the Central Telegraph Office, London, 1871

workers in aviation, shipping and engineering; farmers, motorists, sportsmen, and people on holiday; dwellers in low-lying areas liable to flooding; industrial firms such as makers of ice-cream, and so on. Radio forecasts are second to none because although weather maps are given in the newspapers and on television, they are not as frequent as the weather reports which are broadcast all through the day on radio, and they cannot therefore be so up to date.

A computer at the weather centre sifts out satellite information and also uses reports from weather stations all over the country. The computer compares these details with weather patterns that have been recorded in the past, and shows what the forthcoming weather is likely to be. Skilled meteorologists interpret the findings of the computer, and compile our weather forecasts.

The reports are written at the Central Forecasting Office at Bracknell in Berkshire (where the Meteorological Office has its headquarters) and are sent by teleprinter to the various BBC regions. Special shipping forecasts are given on Radio 2, and cover coastal waters. Gale warnings are broadcast as soon as they are received, even if it means interrupting a radio programme. A forecast of any weather condition that might cause danger to the public, such as a warning of fog, snow, ice or floods, may also interrupt radio or television programmes as a 'news flash'.

A news-room anywhere has news stories coming in all the time from various sources. The editor decides what news shall have priority. Radio news is available at times when there is no programme on television.

Many of the events forming the news are pre-arranged.

For instance, visits of royalty and important political figures, sports meetings, Miss World events and so on are known about and prepared for well in advance. There are always members of staff available to report on special topics, such as parliamentary happenings, and financial, educational and scientific affairs.

'Outside broadcasts' cover television as well as radio, and for television they need what is basically a mobile studio, supplied with electric power and a direct link to a transmitter. This is an expensive set-up, and would not be put in operation for any casual happening. It might be used for some great event that is expected and can be prepared for, or for something important that has already occurred, such as a natural disaster— perhaps a devastating flood.

Some developments from radio can help all classes of users. *Radar* means radio detecting and ranging, and it was developed first in World War II, to detect the presence of enemy aeroplanes. Radio frequencies are sent out, and are reflected back

An early outside radio broadcast. The BBC at the National Rifle Association's Bisley Meeting in 1923

when they meet a solid object. With the help of radar aeroplanes can land safely in darkness, ships can navigate in fog, and blind people can walk along a crowded pavement with confidence.

The walkie-talkie was produced in America in World War II for the use of soldiers, and nowadays it is frequently used by police forces when searching for people who are lost or wanted. It contains a receiver and transmitter, packed in a bag which is slung over the shoulders and carried across the back. As one walks along, one can hold a two-way conversation with others some miles away. A small transistor set, carried in the pocket, is useful in towns or cities, but has a smaller range.

A London policeman speaks to headquarters through a walkie-talkie

7

Camera, Cinema and Television

PHOTOGRAPHY is the art of producing pictures by the action of light on chemically prepared surfaces. It was not discovered by any one man, but was developed from the work of many over hundreds of years.

The earliest form of camera was a plain black box, with a lens at one end and a piece of white glass at the other. Light coming through the lens brought an image of what was outside the lens, and threw this image on to the white glass. The camera got its name from the ancient *camera obscura*, meaning dark room. Probably the camera obscura was discovered by accident. You might be able to produce one for yourself. Imagine a very dark room, with shutters over all the windows, and with bright sunshine outside. If there is a tiny hole in one of the shutters, letting in a beam of light, and a light-coloured room wall opposite the shutter, the image of everything outside that shuttered window will be brought in

An early camera obscura, showing the view from outside in reverse

Opposite: A Victorian family group posed for a photograph

by the light, and will be projected on to the wall. People walking, trees, whatever is outside will appear on the wall upside down.

Ancient showmen used the camera obscura to amuse the crowds. A tent or hut erected on the top of a hill would have a lens placed in a hole in the roof. The light coming through the lens would be reflected by a mirror on to a white table in the middle of the hut, giving an image of everything outside, the whole landscape in miniature. There is a camera obscura on the Downs at Bristol in England. To look at Bristol through it is like looking at a living map.

By the end of the 18th century scientists were experimenting with those chemicals which are sensitive to light, and were taking black and white pictures. Early in the 19th century the

56

Frenchman J. N. Niepce was joined by Louis Daguerre, a
French painter, and together they produced the first photographs. It was Daguerre who, by sheer accident, discovered
that the vapour of mercury would develop photographs.

When families went along to be photographed in those early
days it was not the simple procedure that we know today.
The group would be arranged carefully and set rigidly in
position. Sometimes they were even propped up at the back.
They would have to sit motionless for a long time while the
film was being exposed. The slightest movement resulted in a
blurred picture. Probably it was only the distinction of being
photographed by the famous Daguerre that made it worthwhile
to put up with such discomfort. After a time his pictures were
called 'daguerrotypes'.

Soon the roll film camera was produced, and amateurs began to try their hands at photography. When all the film had been exposed the camera, with the film still loaded in it, had to be returned to the maker. Then the film was removed, processed, and returned with the camera containing a new film.

To obtain a moving picture, a series of photographs must be taken rapidly on a long strip. When this strip is projected on to a screen, we can see movement. In fact, it is the strip which is moving, but our eyes tell us incorrectly that the movement is being made by people or things on the film. Early moving pictures were produced by Thomas Edison (1847–1931), the American inventor of the gramophone, the microphone and the incandescent lamp. Others were working on the project at the same time.

Up to 1928 all cinema films were silent. Captions were flashed on the screen to explain the action, although it was fairly obvious. Those early films look jerky and strange to us today. Great progress was made in the cinema after the invention of the talkies and of colour filming.

Before the days of television, an anonymous writer visualised the possibilities which lay ahead, and wrote, 'If television progresses . . . you may sit by your radio set . . . and may watch all the play in a football match, instead of merely listening to someone describing it. You may sit by a fire in your house . . . and enjoy a play in London. It all sounds impossible and of course it may remain impossible, on any large scale.'

It did sound impossible, but after experiments by early inventors the Scotsman J. L. Baird was able to demonstrate the first true television in London in 1926. His opposite number in the United States, C. F. Jenkins, was working along the same lines. We take television so much for granted that we are unable to realise that less than forty years ago no one of the general public dreamed of having his own television set. Many people in those days had no radio either.

In 1936 the BBC in London started a programme of television for the public. America followed five years later. During World War II (1939–45) restrictions were placed on the manufacture of television receiving sets, and it was not until the war was over that television was able to develop. Today you can have your own choice of programme on your favourite channel. You may prefer comedy, documentary, serious commentaries on the news, plays, classic music or pop music. Television probably takes over a large chunk of your spare time.

Astronaut Edwin Aldrin walks on the surface of the moon. Neil Armstrong's reflection is seen in his face mask

8

The Post Office today

WE have seen how the Post Office came into being, and developed into an important service. Since the end of World War II many modern inventions and techniques have been introduced by the British Post Office to help to cope with the enormous increase in the number of letters sent and received today.

In the past, the sorting of mail in Britain was carried out by hand. Today mechanisation (the use of machines) is gradually taking over most of the labour. Trained men and women work the machines.

Many more letters are posted to catch the outgoing evening mail than at any other time. This is understandable, as business men need to have their desks cleared of letters at the end of the day. For the Post Office, this means that overnight and early in the morning an enormous quantity of letters and packets arrive to be sorted and sent out in the shortest possible time.

At the largest London sorting offices, some of the incoming mail is brought by vans to the arrival platform. Some comes by the underground railway. This underground railway is the only one of its kind in the world; the Post Office is fortunate that it was planned as long ago as in 1909, and has been running since 1927. The cost of building the railway then was only a fraction of what it would be today.

The trains have no drivers; the tunnels are too low and the trains too small for a man to travel on them. They are run by automatic remote control, from control points. In some places the railway is 60 feet below ground, under the Tube railway, and it is 6½ miles long, running from Paddington to the Post Office's Eastern District Central Office at Whitechapel. There are 8 stations and about 60 trains, which travel at 35 miles per hour when they are in the tunnels. The trains carry about 33,000 bags of mail a day.

Sacks of mail, already sorted, have come down the spiral chutes on to the platform, and are waiting in containers to be wheeled on to the train. They are sent on to other stations, and from thence to their final destination. In a matter of half a

Parcel sorting office in Northamptonshire, beside the main railway line. A wheeled container full of bags is waiting for the train

*Containers of mail being loaded on to a train at a station
of the Post Office Underground railway*

minute, the mail is loaded, or off-loaded, and the train rumbles
on again. In the control cabin, the exact position of the train
can be seen all the time.

The underground railway operates for 22 hours out of the 24,
allowing 2 hours daily for maintenance. When an engineer
goes down into the tunnel on repair work, he first switches off
the current by removing a special safety master key (which goes
into his pocket). This puts out an orange light, and shows
that the current has been switched off.

When parcels arrive at one of the mechanised offices they
are carried by a series of conveyors to the sorting machines.
An operator presses a button on a keyboard and directs the
parcel on the belt conveyor to the correct chute and so to the
mail bag according to its destination. Letters and packets,
however, are emptied into a trough which feeds a giant drum,
called a segregator. This drum revolves and separates the
letters from the packets. The packets are then sorted by hand.

The letters are automatically divided into four streams and stacked according to size (all within the Post Office Preferred range, which means the sizes of envelope preferred by the Post Office). At this stage they pass to a machine called ALF, short for Automatic Letter Facing Machine. First Alf turns the letters so that all the stamps are at the bottom, facing the same way.

The 3p stamp has a phosphor band down each side; the $2\frac{1}{2}$p stamp has one phosphor band down the middle. Alf can distinguish between these bands, and separates the mail into first and second class. If only a $\frac{1}{2}$p stamp has been put on the envelope, it goes in with the first class items, because the $\frac{1}{2}$p stamp has two phosphor bands. However, this understamped item would be picked out during primary sorting, and would be surcharged, because it was insufficiently stamped.

After the mail has been separated the stamps are cancelled and it is stacked into piles of first and second class letters. Alf can handle 20,000 an hour. They pass from Alf either to automatic sorting machines or to sorting fittings; at the latter

ALF, the automatic letter facing and stamp cancelling machine. An operator is about to feed letters into it

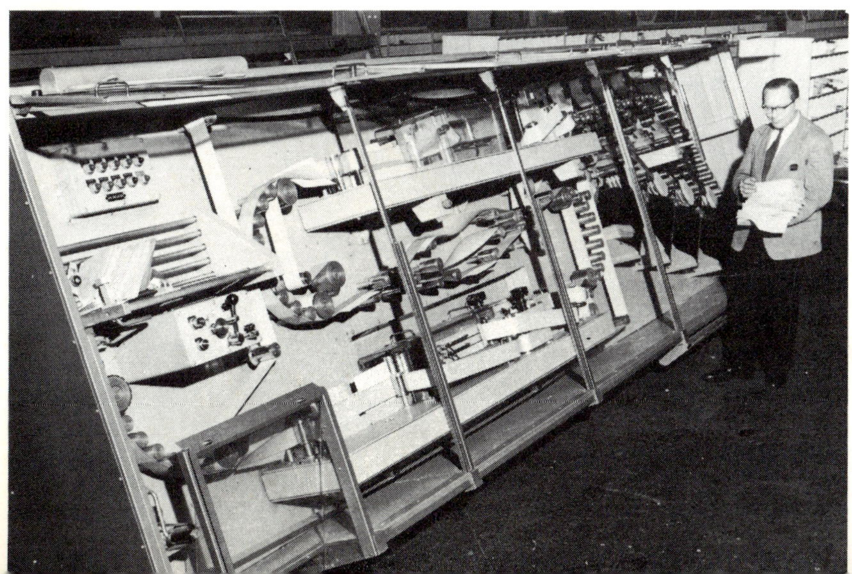

the letters are sorted by hand into main divisions of counties, groups of counties, and the largest towns. This is known as primary sorting, and it is followed by secondary sorting, when the letters are tied into bundles ready to be sent off to their destinations. All the equipment on the sorting floors can be used for both incoming and outgoing traffic, as needed.

Postcodes on letters are important, as they help your mail to be delivered much more quickly. The illustration below shows what happens to postcoded letters. The top letter has the code 1DP, the bottom one has DE1 8ZL. The postman is working on a keyboard similar to that of a typewriter. As each letter drops down in front of him automatically, he types the code on the keyboard and a pattern of harmless phosphorescent dots is printed on the envelope.

The postcodes are usually divided into two blocks of letters and figures. The first block indicates the town or area to which the letter is to be sent. The second block represents the street and sometimes even the actual building within

*An operator at work on
a coding desk machine*

that town or area. The phosphorescent dots enable a letter to be machine sorted at every stage of its journey right up to the postman who delivers it.

The trunk telephone service in Britain began in the year 1884 with the first trunk line from London to Brighton. Today international exchange operators can dial direct to other exchanges almost all over the world. It is now possible for British subscribers in six major cities (London, Liverpool, Birmingham, Manchester, Edinburgh and Glasgow) to dial direct to the major European countries and to the USA (excluding Alaska and Hawaii).

The latest submarine cable can carry as many as 1,840 conversations at the same time. Repeaters, a few miles from each other along the route, are necessary for this service. An invention called TASI has doubled the number of calls that can be made and is being used on older, small capacity submarine cables. TASI is short for a difficult phrase that really is a mouthful—Time Assignment Speech Interpolation.

An international telephone exchange

An artist's impression of the new satellite aerial at Goonhilly in Cornhill

In the ordinary way, two speech channels are provided; one carries outward speech, the other carries inward speech.

You might think that if you have a telephone conversation with someone, you take it in turns to speak, and that all the conversation time is filled up by one or other of you speaking. This is not the case; one of you may ask a question, and there may be a slight pause for thought before the answer comes. In fact, 60% of the time is not used for speech by either of you. This is where TASI comes in, for it takes the unused time on a speech channel and uses it for a conversation between two other people, without in any way interrupting *your* conversation. The Post Office tells us to visualise the speech channel as a pipeline, full of a continuously moving flow of voices talking, which TASI sorts out into the various separate conversations.

In April 1965 the first commercial telecommunications satellite was successfully launched and placed in orbit some 22,300 miles above the equator over the Atlantic ocean region. The satellite, which became known as *Early Bird*, was capable of receiving and transmitting all forms of telecommunications

66

traffic. It provided a service between Europe and America, via specially designed and constructed earth stations sited in France, Germany, and Goonhilly in Cornwall, and via the United States earth station at Andover in Maine.

During the next few years, more satellites were built and launched. They were of improved design, and were able to carry more traffic. At the same time, new earth stations were built in other countries, whilst at Goonhilly a second aerial was built, and a third is under construction in 1972. By mid 1969 the satellite system provided a global service.

High frequency radio is used to provide a telephone service to those countries that cannot be reached either by cable or by satellite. Radio telephony is also used to provide a telephone service to ships at sea.

The Post Office Tower in London was built to improve trunk telephone services, and also to provide for future television services. A new radio technique known as the micro-wave system had been tried out. This system transmits wide-band signals on very small wave-lengths, which can carry 1,800 telephone calls on a single carrier wave.

Post Office Tower, London

Today messages for any country in the world can be sent by Telex, or dictated as a *phonogram* by telephone.

Telex is an exchange service, just like the telephone service, but instead of telephones it uses teleprinters. A teleprinter is a machine which types messages to another teleprinter at a distant point. In Great Britain Telex subscribers—people who rent teleprinters—can send messages to and receive them from any other Telex subscriber in the country and in many countries abroad. The British Telex subscriber just dials the Telex number of the subscriber he wants on the inland system, or on most of the Telex systems in Europe. In case of difficulty, and on calls to some countries outside Europe, the subscriber asks the operator to help him.

When the subscriber is connected to the person he wants, he types a message on his teleprinter; this message appears instantaneously on the teleprinter at the end of the line, and replies can be typed back to the caller. When it is day-time in one country it is night-time in others. As you go east you are losing time; when travelling west, you are gaining time.

Telex operator at work on a teleprinter

Thus you might want to telephone another country from London during the day, only to realise that the person you wish to speak to is in bed in the middle of the night. With Telex, a message can be recorded automatically at the receiving end during night or day, as long as the teleprinter there is switched on to receive messages.

Many of the Post Office services mentioned above are manned by operators. There are also automatic telephone exchanges, which make it possible for you to dial the telephone number you want direct. Trunk or long distance calls can be dialled by most people over the Subscriber Trunk Dialling (STD) system. A code beginning with 'O' connects you to the robot equipment which directs your call. The illustration below gives an idea of what an automatic telephone exchange looks like; the cables come up through the floor, and the top section of the picture is the part that you would see if you walked into the room.

Sectional drawing of an automatic telephone exchange

The Post Office welcomes visitors at many of its important centres. If you have a telephone exchange or a large sorting office near your home ask a grown-up (a relation of yours or your teacher) if a group visit can be arranged with the Head Postmaster.

In London, some of the large buildings which you can visit are:

Faraday Building and *Wren House*, where there are international exchanges. Visits can be arranged through The Reception Room, Faraday Building, Queen Victoria Street, London EC4 4BU.

Fleet Building, 40 Shoe Lane, London EC4A 3DD, the centre for London Inland Telegraphs. Here you can see perforated tapes coming out of the machines, with holes in the tapes which make words. Perhaps your guide will translate messages on them for you. The international Telex exchange is also in Fleet Building, and at St Bodolphs, Bishopsgate, London EC3.

Electra House, Victoria Embankment, London WC2, where there are world-wide telegraph services.

A visit to any of these buildings will take roughly two hours, and an appointment should be asked for about three weeks in advance.

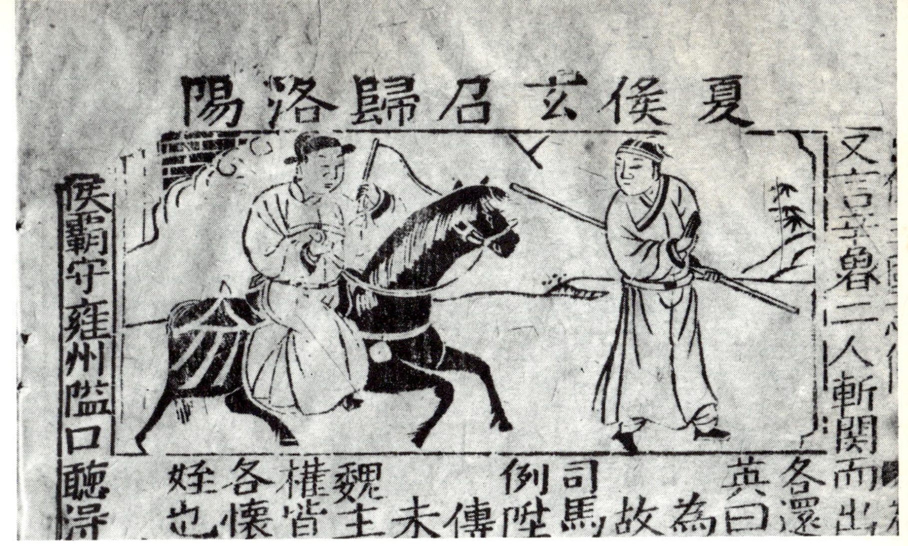

*From a Chinese historical novel, 'The Romance of the Three Kingdoms',
printed from wood-blocks in the 16th century (see page 26)*

Acknowledgements

The author warmly thanks Mr J. A. Hume of the Postal Headquarters
Publicity Branch for his unfailing help and courtesy in arranging many
visits to various Post Office departments; also Miss Jackie Kersley and
their colleagues, who gave so much assistance.

The publishers are most grateful to the following bodies and individuals
for permission to reproduce the illustrations.

Bodleian Library, page 71 (Vet. Or. d. Chin. 91, fol. 23 verso), and
73 (MS Douce 366, fol. 38); British Museum, 13 (lower), 16, 23, 37;
British Tourist Authority, 17; Commissioner of Police for the Metropolis,
v, 54; The Dean and Chapter of Hereford Cathedral and F. C. Morgan,
27; Alte Pinakothek Munich, 1; Victor Gollancz Ltd, 51 (from *Our
Mothers* by Alan Bott); Italian Institute of Culture, 39; Keystone Press
Agency Ltd, 44; London Express Features, 59; Mansell Collection, 24;
Marconi Company Ltd, 50; Oxford University Press, 21; Pitt Rivers
Museum, 10; Post Office, ii, iii, 36, 47, 49, 61, 62, 63, 64, 65, 66, 67, 68,
69; Radio Times Hulton Picture Library, vi, 14, 22, 34, 42, 53, 57;
Reuters Ltd, iv, 43; John Ray, 28; Science Museum, 29, 56; Swiss
National Tourist Office, 8, 9, 32.

Index

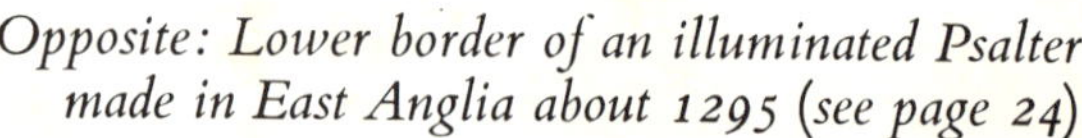
*Opposite: Lower border of an illuminated Psalter
made in East Anglia about 1295 (see page 24)*